Life is too Short

(A Self-Help Book)

Gracia Kasanda Mubala

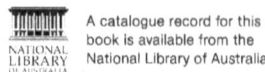 A catalogue record for this book is available from the National Library of Australia

Copyright © 2022 Gracia Kasanda Mubala
All rights reserved.
ISBN: 978-1-922727-49-7

Linellen Press
265 Boomerang Road
Oldbury, Western Australia
www.linellenpress.com.au

Dedication

I dedicate this book to young people and honour my late sister Noela Kasanda God'swill, who passed away shortly before I finished writing this book. Thank you for being the sister that you were, an inspiration to the family and the body of Christ. Rest in glory, dear sister.

Contents

Dedication iii

Contents v

Preface 1

Introduction 3

Chapter 1 - Life is a Journey 6

Chapter 2 - Life is a mystery 9

Chapter 3 - Life is an adventure! 14

Chapter 4 - A Quality Life 15

Chapter 5 - The mind 19

Chapter 6 - Wisdom is profitable to direct 21

My vision in life 22

Conclusion 26

About the Author 27

Preface

'Life is too short' is a common phrase. In life, it is easy to get carried away by temporal and perishable things while putting the real and relevant things on hold, even procrastinating. For a long time, people have been living as though the world would never end. Even though the world seems like it will never end, it does. It ends for individuals at some point in time.

There are things that make humans acknowledge that life is short. For instance, the world has been moved by events such natural disasters, deadly disease and, since 2019, the Corona Virus pandemic. My mentor once said: *"As the Lord wills, a lot of people have plans, but as long as people don't totally depend on God, then there's a problem. People have to know that God's will supersedes their plans. So, always say as God wills because for those who call the name of the Lord, he'll heal their land. There's nothing that happens without God knowing. Families need to spend time together, share among one another and draw near to God."*

What a statement!! For sure, God said if my people who are called by name shall humble themselves and seek my face, I will forgive their sins and heal their land. The world system has been affected and changed in a twinkle of an eye: travelling restrictions; at one point, toilet tissue became as valuable as gold; the uncertainty of tomorrow, and so on and so forth. Until such events happen, human beings tend to put the real and valuable things on hold or compromise to be accepted in society.

While you have the ability to be in control, value yourself, value your loved ones (family), show compassion and then you will matter. When I first got the inspiration to write this book, I wasn't in accord with it. However, when I started writing the book, a certain event unfolded and shook me. It's like a curtain opened for me to see that life on earth is indeed too short. It also made me value the quality of life rather than the quantity of life.

Introduction

Why is it that the world is full of people who are confused – confused about so many things? The world is full of mothers who are unsure of how to manage their homes and children; fathers who are lost in thoughts but don't know the right decisions to make. We have people who are unsure of which direction to take in life, what career to choose, whether to be with a particular business partner or spouse. The truth of the matter is that, when there is no revelation, there's no direction. Revelation in life brings about the knowledge and wisdom one needs to solve and handle certain issues.

Genesis 1:2 "Now the earth was formless and empty, darkness was over the surface of the deep, and the Spirit of God was hovering over the waters".

Life is like a journey. We may all be in the same bus, but our bus stop differs. We may all be driving on the same highway, but our exit points differ depending on the destination. I had a funny experience. Well, it is now, not then. Upon arriving in Australia, I started high school. My case worker showed me the bus to take me to and from school. He also mentioned the other buses that passed along the same road to my house. After my first day of school, I met some church youth who went to the same school. They assured me that the bus they were catching would drive around my suburb, so I joined them. While on the bus, I realised that the bus was driving past our then church premises. I panicked because I knew that we'd already passed my house. I hopped off the bus and wandered the suburb for almost an hour, but, if I knew the area well, it would only take less than twenty minutes to get home. It was getting late, my parents were getting worried, stopping every bus they saw to check for me. When I arrived home, I thanked God in my heart that I didn't lose my family in a new and strange land. But at the same time, I was angry because my parents were yelling at me ….

When I was in Africa, I knew every corner to turn to take me home but not in a new country. Everything was new. I was also new to myself. I was trying to integrate and find out how effective my character and personality would fit in a new land. It was a long journey to get where I am today. That's life, isn't it? Life is full of challenges and obstacles.

Sometimes we enter other people's worlds, get carried away and forget who we are, where we are coming from and where we are going in life. My purpose was to go to school and return home safely. Making friends was a bonus. But after being carried away, I wasted most of the time wondering, chatting and wandering the streets trying to find my house. Some of us find ourselves wandering and wasting time in environments where our purpose is not relevant. As a result, we get frustrated by rejection and negative experiences.

Chapter 1

Life is a Journey

Our life journey begins far away from our knowledge. (God said to Jeremiah, *"Before I formed you in your mother's womb, I knew you"*). But the moment we land on earth, into our parents' hands, we begin a long journey on earth. My story of being lost relates to a lot of people in a way, because when we come on earth as babies, everything is strange. When babies begin to gain consciousness of themselves, they begin to realise that there's a lot to learn. And so, they begin to adapt. As they grow, they begin to experiment, ask many questions, and discover what is and what is not.

In early stages of life, we learn about our traditions, cultures, education, values and beliefs. These things have a huge impact on how we journey in life. From a young age, if traditions bind us to things that are positive and pleasant, we enjoy life better. On the other hand, if our traditions bind us to negativity, it limits our expression and enjoyment in life. This book is written to draw the reader's attention to this. No matter your traditional beliefs and culture, know that your satisfaction in this short life lies in applying what you know.

> WE CAN LEARN SO MUCH IN THIS LIFE
> BUT IF WE DON'T PRACTICE
> WHAT WE LEARN,
> THE KNOWLEDGE BECOMES USELESS

For instance, I sacrificed my sweat and energy in education. I have completed many courses but still struggled to get or create employment for myself. One day, my boss told me that I study a lot but do not make use of my studies. I was denied a position because I hadn't practised in my profession for many years. I am not writing to blame my former boss or defend myself, rather to show the importance of applying knowledge.

> *John 14:21 - The one who loves me is the one who keeps my Commandments*

Life is a journey in itself.

And life is a journey full of obstacles. While we are on this journey, there are things and spirits trying to impose or cooperate with us. More than a building, fellowship or gathering of believers, a church is a spiritual place where things of the spirit happen. In the realm of the spirit, there is always contention, contention between angels and demons who don't want the manifestation of things. Physical life is a report card of what's happening in the spirit. On the life journey, two spirits want me – God and the Devil.

From personal experience, I have met evil, undecided, unpredictable and wise friends.

> *Often in life we deal with the same characters but different faces.*

In life, we need to develop the ability to quickly identify the character of those around us and use wisdom in relating with them.

Truly wise friends are rare. Some relationships take advantage of others so it is advisable to leave such kind of relationships as soon as you find out, lest they affect your motion in life. Life is just like a bus. We get on this bus alone and get down alone. While on the life-bus, be conscious to make friends who will positively impact the lives of those we meet on the life-bus, and vice versa. The positive impacts take us a long way, while the negative impact may discourage us. This self-help book is written to help the reader make the most out of this life journey.

Chapter 2

Life is a mystery

From infancy, it's hard to know what's going on inside a human brain. The mystery of life is that there is more to what we see. "Don't judge a book by its cover". Life is not just physical, but also spiritual. In life, you have to work hard to get what you want or deserve. Sometimes people do work hard but don't get what they worked for. Some don't get what they deserve. Others say that life doesn't give you what you deserve but what you demand.

I used to believe that the spirit world exists, but I didn't believe that the spirit world had an impact on the physical world until I met my husband. Later on, my husband and I joined Jesus Prayer and Power ministry (church). It is then that I began to discover a lot about the spiritual side of life through teachings and deliverances. I have also discovered a lot through real-life testimonies from people who were members of secret cults. They explain the importance of praying at midnight, how spiritual transactions are made to steal and hijack destinies. Crafty people use evil spiritual means to destroy lives.

Ephesians 3:9 says: "And to bring to light for everyone what is the plan of the mystery hidden for ages in God who created all things".

From verse 1, Apostle Paul speaks about the mysteries of Christ, which was not known to people in previous generations, only to a few, but is now revealed to us by the Holy Spirit. There are many things that hinder or quicken our manifestation in life. The main thing that hinders or quickens our motion in life is knowledge. Knowledge is power. Life mystery also lies in how well our beliefs, education and traditions are. Some traditions limit people from living their best.

In Ephesians 3:4, Paul talks about understanding and insight. And Jesus talks about knowing the truth, and the truth shall set you free. Before man was made into a physical being, He was the first spirit before He formed them out of the dust, created in God's nature, then formed into a being. But for a better frequency, God created the bridge between the spiritual and the physical man, which is the mind. It is hard to live on earth and matter when you are not spiritually awakened.

Even as a born-again Christian, or a medical doctor, you have to practice what you know. By doing this, you will remain relevant in life. It takes more than motivation, passion and a positive attitude to journey well. It also takes wisdom and the right relationships to live well. In this life journey, you need to ensure that the ones you carry along are true friends; true friends can make you matter in life. Iron sharpens iron. Friends or people who are happy to celebrate, encourage and even rebuke you will help you go a long way in life; will help you even live long.

> *Then God said, "Let us make mankind in our image, in our likeness so that they may rule over the fish in the sea and the birds in the sky, over the livestock and all the wild animals, and over all the creatures that move along the ground.*
>
> *So God created mankind in His own image, in the image of God He created them*
>
> *Genesis 1:26 & 27*

I always wondered why people seek higher powers, mostly negative powers, to acquire wealth status and so on. I also noticed that churches are packed, although people may not be fully planted but are attracted to that particular church because there are wonders, miracles and prophecy. I must admit that I was among those that said people prefer prophecy to the word of God. But later in life, I discovered I needed both the word of God and prophecy for edification and direction.

It's comforting to hear from my maker and His thoughts towards me. He said to Jeremiah:

"I know the thoughts that I think towards you, saith the Lord, thoughts of peace and not of evil, to give you an expected end. (Jeremiah 29:11).

My pursuit for spiritual understanding is based on wanting to know what is blocking me from running smoothly in life. What is the cause behind particular repetitive negative patterns in my life, which happen mostly around the same time of the year. Then I came across Jesus Prayer and Power ministry. I have come a long way and still have a long way to go. Unless you know what is blocking you in life, your life will forever be miserable.

There are covenants that were made in families far back before you were born. There might be secrets parents hide from children and did not address them. Now those secrets are hunting their children today. Until those secrets are exposed and addressed, they will keep on costing those who are born in that bloodline.

This life mystery is what causes people to seek prophets. It is the one who is in need of the doctor that will seek the doctor. Don't judge others quickly because there is more than what we see. Instead of judging the person, ask: "What else could it be?" because an unanswered question will always remain a problem.

Once you are connected to the Holy Spirit and be your BFF, in one way or another, He will expose the spiritual instructions on how to handle certain issues, where to go, who to go to, what and what not to say. Then you will enjoy the life journey on earth and in your environment to the fullest.

The best thing the Holy Spirit is teaching me now is self-control. Life is like driving a car. To qualify as a driver, you need self-control, the fruit of the Spirit. With self-control, you will avoid traps, slow down on life's road bumps; you will control your temper and many other things. Open your eyes and ears to the things of the spirit, not evil spirit, so you can overcome in life.

Chapter 3

Life is an adventure!

Life is an adventure! I'm not a risk taker, but I do take risks, to some extent. Sometimes, life is enjoyable when you are open-minded. Try new things, change a career or even make an investment. Some things look hard until you try them. Some people look like they are not good until you get close to them. Be open-minded to ideas, people and many other things.

When I was younger, I used to say that I would not get married. Later in life, that idea changed, but I had decided in my heart not to have children because I use to think deep. I didn't like the idea of children suffering, going through pains and challenges, until I got into marriage. Now I enjoy my relationship, but I enjoy more the fact that I'm a mother. It's a delight to say that the Lord has blessed me with blessed and anointed children. I learn from my children; they challenge me to do some things that I wouldn't have done if I didn't have them. I am thankful to God for allowing me to experience life from this angle.

Chapter 4

A Quality Life

Life is too short, and to make the most out of this life, you need to plan; you need to know where you are going. This will give you a quality life rather than a wasted life.

How to live a quality life is a matter of personal decision, based on your purpose and what you want to achieve in life. The one who enjoys and lives a quality life is the one who puts on an attitude of not letting the negative pull them down. It is easier said than done, but it is also possible if you train yourself.

A quality life is also accompanied by self-discipline and self-control. Goodness and productivity start with self before they can be spread to others, and this can depended on what made you choose the type of friends, business partners or even love partner. Ask yourself: what do you want to contribute to the society, church and others? Check … does what you do give you peace?

What gives me peace at the end of my day, month or year is based on the application. Decisions and application are what makes us impact others and our surroundings. There are people in this world who know what is right for them. They know what triggers them but don't have enough courage to address it sincerely. They worry about what people will say about them rather than being who they really are. Again, some people know what they are doing is wrong and that it harms their environment, but they have the courage to do it anyway. People need to learn and change their mentality of how they view life and how they address things. It is not bad to address things sincerely, however, do it with respect and in a healthy manner. Some people don't feel valued because they put on hold what is meant to make them valued. Some don't have a clear vision of what they want to achieve in life. I write to encourage you, the reader, to gain control of your life and make your life journey more satisfying. You will not get lost in things or relationships if you are in control and allow God to lead and guide you. Work hand in hand with God on the life-bus. Realign with your purpose each time you realise that you are going astray. Life is too short to waste the valuable lessons of life's adventure.

I watched a movie called *Inside a Living Body from Birth to Death* and I acknowledged that life is indeed a journey, and a timed one as well. Even when we look after ourselves, eat well and so on, as we age, our body cells will eventually shut down. Therefore, it is important to have a clear mission and action plan; have a routine that you can follow in accordance with the current season and self-investment. Self-investment is very important.

A quality life is a result of :

- ➢ self-discipline - Be disciplined in what you do or say. Motivation or having a vision without and action is a vision by name only.

- ➢ The power of Self Expression. Self-expression has its positives and negatives. Positively, it gives you the opportunity to get off your chest words, ideas and actions. It also allows you to review your words and actions so you can make changes, if necessary, which leads to growth and emotional maturity. Self-expression is both words and actions. There's a quote that says: *Value a person by their actions and you will not be fooled by their words.*

    Jesus said: *Let your Yes be Yes and No be No.* When people are not given the opportunity to truly express themselves, they can become toxic and hypocritical.

- ➢ Words are also powerful - Bridle your tongue. Life and death lie in the tongue. Don't just declare positively to my environment; cover the entire globe. Every decision made by governments affects us, following the laws of the land. A quality life is a result of considering many things. Even the opportunity to express yourself should not be misused.

- ➢ Emotional maturity is the key in this life journey. When you are leader, parent or influencer in this life, you need to work on emotional maturity. It comes with a lot of patience and experience.

As mentioned in the previous chapter, life is a mystery and the spirit controls the physical. It's important to look after yourself holistically, that is, looking after your body, soul and spirit.

The body: what do you eat, physical exercise and good rest and good hygiene. Our body functioning is at the mercy of what we put into ourselves. When we are stressed, thinking a lot, we begin to lose weight and feel tired.

The Soul: what do you feed your mind by what you watch, hear and speak. Your eyes and eyes are the window to your soul. Jesus said *we are destroyed by not what we put in but by what comes out*. Matthews 15: 11 and verse 8.

Spirituality: the best way to be spiritually connected or awakened is by allowing yourself to be led by the Holy Spirit. We must be very conscious of allowing the Holy Spirit to lead us. Once we allow the Holy Ghost to lead us, we'll realise that we have given Him absolute control, even in a familiar way. Sometimes we may come across a roadblock then we need to tune to the GPS – who is the Holy Ghost – so that we do not waste time going around.

Chapter 5

The mind

A successful life begins in the mind. Google's definition of a mind is "the element of a person that enables them to be aware of the world and their experiences, to think, feel: the faculty of consciousness and thought."

When the mind is in darkness and ignorance, it makes a person confused. Have you heard of the saying: "An idle mind is the devil's workshop"? On many occasions, when a person has no knowledge of certain things, they tend to be confused or feel out of place – at school, work, church or even in a relationship. A prince who is aware of his status acts out of confidence. He can use his authority to change rules, make orders and many more. On the other hand, a prince who is not aware of his status may live at the mercy of his servants.

To be successful, you need to take time and check your mindset. How? By checking the kind of thoughts you entertain, how you view your world and the world at large. You can also check your mindset by the decisions you make. Do the decisions you make give you and those around your peace?

The Bible says in proverbs 23:7 *"As a man thinketh in His heart, so is he"*.

A corrupt mind brings about corrupted results.

It is important to look after the mind, just as it's important to look after our health. Just as we keep a balanced diet, eat and drink well, we need to feed our mind the right information. God said to the dark world, *"Let there be light"* and there was light. It is when the light was on that God began to put things in order. This is to show us that when we feed our minds with the right information, it begins to enlighten our minds. A well-informed mind makes correct and sound decisions.

I would like to bring in a personal experience. In the past, I was unsure of certain information. With some, I had some information but not all the information. This brought about confusion. However, when I was educated and received a clear revelation of that information, I had peace of mind … till today. Why? It's because now my actions and decision run on the foundation of that information.

A successful life also depends on how well our mind operates. Positive confessions also lead to a successful life. People speak what they ponder or think about in the mind, whether it's a lie or truth.

Chapter 6

Wisdom is profitable to direct

The previous chapter discusses the impact of an informed, educated, and knowledgeable mind. Knowledge brings about revelation. What is wisdom? Wisdom is simply the correct application of knowledge. There are many good things the bible says about wisdom. Things such as:

WISDOM IS PROFITABLE TO DIRECT
WISDOM IS BETTER THAN STRENGTH
WISDOM IS BETTER THAN WEAPONS OF WAR
BY HIS WISDOM DELIVERED A CITY.

Wisdom is essential to acquire in order to be successful in life, especially when it comes to dealing with people relations and business. With wisdom, you can endure certain things and people in life. You can also sacrifice certain habits for dignity. You can be consistent in your character and dealings. If you are not wise, you can invest wrongly, destroy valuable relations and whatever you have built over the years.

Write your vision(s), missions and make them a prayer point. If you just write visions and missions but do not work towards achieving them then you are wasting your time. Praying over your visions and missions is part of working towards achieving them.

My vision in life

Who am I?

_____
_____

My vision

_____
_____

My mission in life

_____
_____

Objectives (that is, how you want to achieve your vision)

_____
_____

My life destination or where do I want to end up?

_____
_____

The hard one would be my destination. But think of the end of your career: if a parent, what do you want to achieve when your children leave the house, or do you want to spend eternity with Jesus.

What has control over my life?

_____
_____

What controls my thoughts

   Good thoughts

_____

   Bad thoughts

_____

   How can I change them? (Romans 12:2)

_____

What are my achievements/ Failures

_____
_____
_____
_____

Who are my friends?

_____
_____

Below are some of the strategies I have been using since 2018 from my Quiet time, in order to journey well and live a quality life.

> *Motivation speaking will not get you anywhere without action.*
>
> **"Being consistent with God is the KEY!**

> *Purpose in my heart that, no matter how good, there'll always be people that will stone me. But I should stay focused on God*

> *Seeking honour from people creates a lot of turmoil*

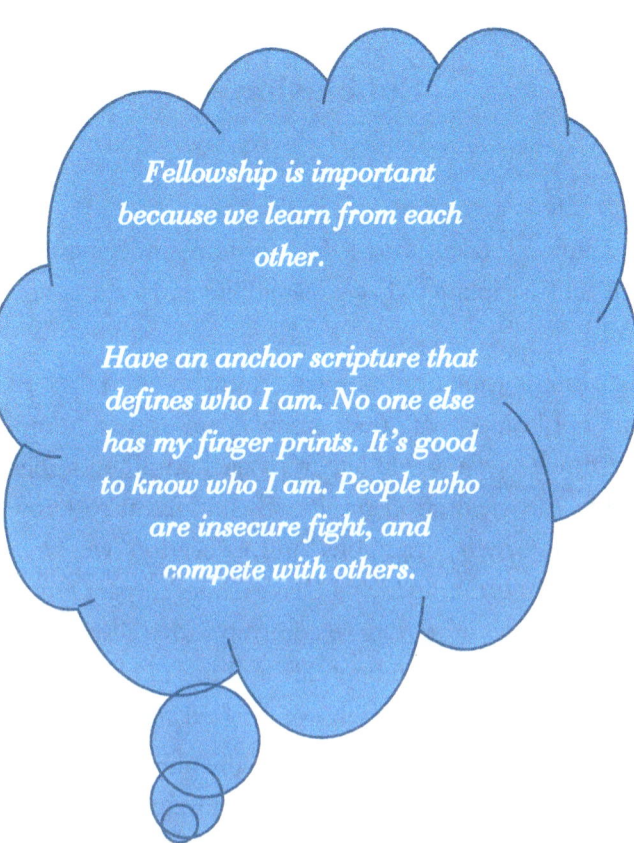

Fellowship is important because we learn from each other.

Have an anchor scripture that defines who I am. No one else has my finger prints. It's good to know who I am. People who are insecure fight, and compete with others.

Conclusion

Life is a journey. Life is a mystery. And life is an adventure. It takes knowledge, wisdom, understanding and self-discipline to live a quality life and a successful life.

Life is too short, so living a quality life relies on the application of that knowledge and wisdom. Inasmuch as we would like to navigate on the journey of life and yield good results, it's important to know that the beliefs, traditions and education we were exposed to earlier in life will have a huge impact on us. Therefore, it's important to come up with a clear vision of where you want to be in life and put in place some good strategies to help achieve the best results.

Life on earth is not limited to the physical but also the spiritual side. Therefore, it's important to create a balance between the two: have spiritual insight on how to overcome and enjoy life here on earth.

About the Author

Gracia Kasanda Mubala is the author of *Seasons Come and Seasons Go But God Never Changes*, and *Ministry and Parenting Challenges*. Her passion lies in helping people discover what matters most in life, using what they have and maximise their potential to live a quality and productive life.

Gracia holds a Bachelor Degree of Commerce, an Advanced Diploma of Counselling and Community Services. She loves to sing, read and write, which has helped her achieve her goal of writing this book.

www.ingramcontent.com/pod-product-compliance
Lightning Source LLC
Chambersburg PA
CBHW070341120526
44590CB00017B/2975